THE OCCUPATION

THE OCCUPATION

Poems by
Jay McCoy

Accents Publishing • Lexington, Kentucky • 2016

Copyright © 2016 by Jay McCoy
All rights reserved

Printed in the United States of America

Accents Publishing
Editor: Katerina Stoykova-Klemer
Cover Image: CSIRO

ISBN: 978-1-936628-39-1
First Edition

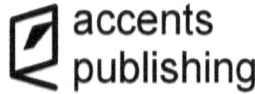

Accents Publishing is an independent press for brilliant voices. For a catalog of current and upcoming titles, please visit us on the Web at

www.accents-publishing.com

CONTENTS

Calling / 1
what it was like for me / 2
Distinguishing Characteristics in Four Polaroids / 3
flattery could get you everything / 4
him / 5
learning to speak your name / 7
your hands / 8
In Other Words / 9
Starvation / 10
Following the Scientific Method to Newton's Second Law / 11
how we became a couple / 12
Two Insomnias / 13
Distilling Ganymede / 14
Apoptosis / 16
Draw / 17
the occupation / 18
Keeping Count / 20
why I'm positive / 21
The Pursuit of Happiness / 23
shadow/boys / 24
biohazard / 27
full blown, when used to modify your condition / 28

Acknowledgments / 29

CALLING

Your voice through
the phone line cracked
on the other end before
you said the first word,

so I knew

what you needed/wanted
to say, but could not yet
wrap your mind around all
possibilities, positive/negative,

so I just waited.

WHAT IT WAS LIKE FOR ME

      in response to tina andry

The first time we did not come to it as naturally
as coalescing Russian nesting dolls. I struggled

to locate trigger points, to align proper parts.
Even now, I may stumble sometimes / never staying

after a second chance encounter. It was not
until I learned my satisfaction depends

upon sacrifice more than suffering, not
until I gave up searching for the forgotten

reminders of all the others
who came before me.

DISTINGUISHING CHARACTERISTICS IN FOUR POLAROIDS

> ... another body sank through the earth's crust
> and we got some good pictures ...
>
> —William Burroughs, *The Soft Machine*

I thought only I knew certain
intimacies of your soft machine:

I

pale flanks slow revealing
cherished childhood scars
constellate with freckles
& fading tattooed stars;

II

ripples peaking from
waistband to just below
navel, becoming more
distinct with ragged breath;

III

hollow lying hidden above
left collar bone, brimming
with sweat—spent
too long in summer sun;

IV

musk-ripe sweet spot manifest
by birthmark—underside right arm
exposed that morning I discovered you
were ticklish to my unkempt chin.

FLATTERY COULD GET YOU EVERYTHING

No, it's not you; it's not that you can't trust
me. I know history will prove I've lived
up to my fast reputation. I'm prone
to give in to attentive affections
& random public advances. I know
I give it away too freely, too soon.
You could never call me a rakish bore,

even when I toss horrible words
so loosely. I've made such a grave
mistake thinking we could survive
my past indiscretions. Maybe you should
move on to someone who cares
for you, someone who knows
truly what a future may hold.

HIM

I

I have seen him before
across the room/bar/next table
talking with a woman, eyes wandering
to meet mine—habitually, he
wets his lips. My mind traces
the landscape of his face.

II

I have seen him before
in black & white, scented/glossy print
magazine ads (of men & women) draped
in rumpled/white cotton garments, salt
water drenching thirsty lines of his body
emerging through waves, rescinding
surf. Rushing/retreating sands
massage his feet/ankles/calves.

III

I have seen him before
in my dreams. Hands caressing neck/shoulders,
exploring chest/arms, venturing south
to warm the small of his back. Drawing
circles from pooling sweat, dragging a river
up his spine toward a full-body kiss—
his skin on mine.

IV

I have seen him before
in other lovers I have had. In my bed
that next morning awakening to stare
at him / wonder about the stories
I haven't been told about former
girlfriends he's afraid to speak
of for fear I may be just like him.
Men (& women) who leave
have left a mark in my body / mind.
Indentions in my soul last longer
than those in my pillows.

LEARNING TO SPEAK YOUR NAME

                                                  you broke me
                                                 in—taught me

                                                how to take it
                                          like a man even

                                          though we were
                                                   only boys

YOUR HANDS

soothe me, searching
for remnants of other

lovers who left
their marks on me—

you search in vain. I do not
allow you to see my scars; I recoil

them inside, nestled comfortably
within my soul—awaiting

their perfectly-timed,
precision-aimed release.

IN OTHER WORDS

Back when Alfalfa was on South Lime,
I would awaken the morning after
a poetry reading with a sweet hangover
to you next to me

                    in my bed, disheveled.
Your eyes, underscored as with ash
even on mornings after you had actually slept,
told me you had to go back to him.

                    I never asked
you to stay. I could never quite
force my lips to form around the *please*
beginning my unspoken request,
so I instead kissed you awake,

                    simply left
it with, *I know you need to go before
he wonders,* even though he always knew
where you were.

                    He could never
admit you were already gone two
years before you said it publicly,
actually left him,
but not for me.

STARVATION

Let me feed on your anger diced into bits, tossed with leaves of romaine, jicama, olives, hearts of palm, traces of a balsamic Dijon-based vinaigrette laced with the lies you spoke. Allow me to drink in your bitterness, ground into morsels, mixed with my morning cup of dark-roasted Ethiopian free-trade beans— their life driven out by sharp steel blades, drowned by scalding water, resuscitated with a side of sugared hopes, creamy dreams, & ice cubes of your alleged innocence. Poison me with your resentment, smothered in a rich burgundy mushroom sauce, disguised as a vegan brisket—carrots, tofu, peppers, fava beans, & onions—a gelatinous mound, once separate ingredients, now solid/strangled into a presentable mass, substantial enough to satisfy my unrequited hunger.

FOLLOWING THE SCIENTIFIC METHOD TO NEWTON'S SECOND LAW

I learn fast

the natural laws underpinning
well-conceived theory that two objects
cannot occupy the same physical area

& remember lucidly the melodic recitation
synchronous as my right ocular socket struggles
to remain intact within my skull

while your clenching metacarpus exerts
its accelerating desire to acquire
my proportional/personal mass.

After all these years, I know all
too well that your sensible hypotheses
& rational explanations

Based upon empirical observations drawn
through rigorous processes will only bring us
to the unavoidable/logical conclusion—

I love you blindly.

HOW WE BECAME A COUPLE

On the first night
we met, you stayed
with me. Only ten days
together, you said
you loved me.

Approaching eight weeks,
you began calling us
a couple. After six months,
you asked me
to move in. I did.

During our first
fight, you lost
your temper—your fist
found my eye. Over
two years, two times

I moved out; twice, you
persuaded my return.
This time you beg me,
Don't leave—threaten
the worst. I do.

TWO INSOMNIAS

Praise God for these two insomnias!
And the difference between them.

—Rumi

I

Between respites
& revelations, I long

for your body melding
with mine.

II

Just beyond
the miter of obsession

& ardor, I discover
my joy returns.

DISTILLING GANYMEDE

> committing no crime but their own wild cooking pederasty and intoxication
>
> —Allen Ginsberg

You begin with full-bodied wine, cold-pressed
from blond twinks who blew and were blown
in the underground garage, bare-assed against cast iron

and concrete, writhing out of mind, out of sight
of bright Aldebaran tracking Seven Sisters, wandering
the Seven Hills. Savor succulent extract rimmed

from the gym-rat ginger's faggot obsession for sinewy
musk seeping from carmine-colored Umbros glanced
askew on cedar benches in the basement steam

room of the Central Parkway YMCA. Simmer long
& hot over pyre with the silver-haired daddy discovered
beneath tin ceilings, smoking Reds, who fucked furiously

out of necessity, because of drunken desire being
caught alone outside Kaldi's at the devil's hour. Blend in
rough trade, if you dare, juicy from bath houses

by abandoned train tracks near the Olentangy, who left
you with twisted taut nipples and rancid residue of palm
prints stained on your cheeks. Boil them all slowly down

with the rolling bug chaser vociferously plowed
on the rooftop under unflinching gaze of Aquarius
and starry-eyed Aquila pausing pensive above

your Queen City. In the end, render every face blank
and every seraphim mouth mute. Leave bejeweled bodies
disjointed, unrecognizably reduced to purgatoried torsos,

to endless cock and balls, beneath a once-mortal moon
reflected in the glistening heady / sweet remnants.

APOPTOSIS

> /apəpˈtōsəs/ *noun* programmed form of cell death leading to the elimination of cells to maintain homeostasis; normal and necessary phenomenon for various biological development processes, allowing cells to differentiate from one another and to form proper connections; excessive or faulty apoptosis is often associated with many disorders and cellular suicide

I remember when such words would have stumbled
from my lips, taken a rolling tumble off my tongue,

or gotten lodged in my throat.

Now, I incorporate terminology I never wanted
to know, internalize vocabulary I never asked to acquire—

replicate them nimbly into my lexicon.

Becoming comfortable with multisyllabic monstrosities
has made me vigilant with acronyms.

DRAW

She must be new. I've never seen her
here before—a vision in white, all
business except when she smiles
her crooked/coy grin, says I have *pretty*

veins. Her hazel eyes hold steady
my gaze as the cold needle plunges
into raised blue lines traversing
the bend of my right arm. *Now*

just hold this tight.

THE OCCUPATION

unbeknownst to us, the occupation began
cascading through morning's heady amyl nitrate fog
through ripple glass of the refurbished mechanic's institute

blinding sunshine accompanies the initial invasion—
dirty-faced angels not awaiting introductions
quietly lay siege—confiscate irreplaceable valuables

preparing for the many battles that will comprise this war,
compose this symphony, when scholars return retrospectively
to catalog the quiet dead & quarantine the poet survivors

foul smells & unholy sights emblazon across countrysides;
red body bags and yellow biohazard tape announce
the coming waves—quick progress slowly discovered

as human technology lags behind viral ingenuity
alphabets disintegrate into letters & indiscernible acronyms
symbiotic cooperation will determine our survival—

bound/tied/gagged/caged into our mundane daily comings
& goings, remembering foregone days without restrictions
abandoning pleasures unabashed, now suffocating

mud & mire warfare waged without knowledge—
but we should have known better
safely educated & penetrated by objects of affection

we preach to one another in morphing doxology
as the language of the invaders changes the feel of our tongues
so they become the foreign bodies lodged in our mouths

forcing our epiglottises to restrict the airflow—
changing shapes of consonants while removing
the offending vowels from our vocabulary

KEEPING COUNT

You gained
187 new CD4 cells, nudged
your percentage just above 20;
your viral load has gone

undetectable. Your meager sanguine
family grew from 421
six months ago to a brood
588 *strong* today—

you don't know
that strong is the right word,
so you don't speculate
on tomorrow, let alone

next year. You resuscitate
your thoughts, reconsider
your position—having less
defines your diagnosis;

if you squander
your bounty below
200, you may graduate
from three letters to four.

WHY I'M POSITIVE

maybe it was the gasping for air
as your lungs collapsed from being

submerged too long
maybe it was the gurgling
sounds as metallic/warm vitality
filled your parched/dry mouth

maybe it was the glaring/dead
eyes looking right through
as you passed out of control
& into your own release

maybe it was the gaping loneliness
waiting on the other side of you

maybe it was the grinding
metal on bone/after steel
tore flesh with your arms left
flailing on the hardwood floor

maybe it was the sight of dried blood
caked around olfactory exit wounds
reflected in that too white/too
sanitary/perfectly-tiled chamber

maybe it was the confused morning
you awoke in that pungent bed

exposed/stripped bare after
a suffocating night/seroconversion

maybe it was eyes welling up
& lacrimal dams bursting

like cheap plastic pools succumbing
to the frenzied weight of a stagnant
August afternoon or maybe/just
maybe he did love you

I don't know why
he cried but he did

THE PURSUIT OF HAPPINESS

> Intuition and impulse are extraordinarily important things in life;
> you will not be well-served if the impulse is shut down or you
> think about everything too much. Sometimes you just do it.
>
> —John Littig

Some days end

        in your brownstone
on the couch holding hands with your life
partner who's a life coach like you,
but most days,

        there's no bag
over your head to keep the helium
at maximum concentration. A certain
First Lady once said you should
do one thing every day
that scares you,

        but I don't
think this is the *scary*
she had in mind.

SHADOW/BOYS

I walk home through shadows
stretching endlessly—watching
lovers on a park bench entwined
in that primal ritual falsely called
love—it's sex—it's only love
when you mean it

crossing intersections
regardless of the *don't walk* signs
& red lights

(red light means stop)

stop this madness
stop the darkness—turn on the (day)lights
stop, look both ways

people on the corner shrouded
in darkness, bathed in the night/river
flooded with street lights soon doused out
with tagged spray paint or a rock
       conveniently tossed upward to darken
       the moth-attracting yellow light

(yellow light means yield)

yield to (on)coming traffic
yield to your passions
yield to observe

men meeting women
men meeting men
for money
for drugs
for ecstasy
for sex
for fantasy that may last
fo(u)r days in your mind
       but only se(co)nds in your guilt

men losing sight
of (their) young children
at home with wives who believe stories
about late-night poker games
about nights on the town with the *boys*
       (jailbait/beautiful) boys, still exploring—
       not sure

of themselves—not sure
of their lives—not sure
of you
       sure of your (needs)
sure of your wants
sure of your money
at the end of a cold hard fuck

(green light means go)

go home to (your) wife
go home to (your) children

go home to suburbia
go home

        make a donation
        to a late-night call-in show
        get these boys off
        the streets—save their souls

calm your conscience

BIOHAZARD

You only become
dangerous when you die.

                                              I'm positive

I have been toxic throughout
my life—a health hazard
requiring safety precautions

previously retired/reserved
for lethally uneducated
masses, now resurrected.

FULL BLOWN, *WHEN USED TO MODIFY YOUR CONDITION*

You tell yourself, *keep quiet; hold your tongue.* You really don't think she means anything with her choice of adjectives. In fact, you don't know that she even considers not saying it the way she did. You've grown numb to rampant insensitivity & indifference that most people show. You chalk it up to her lack of exposure. You guess it's the same thing that got you here in the first place.

ACKNOWLEDGMENTS

Thanks to my parents who always have encouraged me to forge my own path and have given their unconditional love whether I have soared or stumbled along my life's journey.

Thanks to the creative community that is Lexington and Kentucky for nurturing my words & my spirit over so many years with special thanks to my kin by choice from Poezia, the Appalachian Writers Workshop, Holler Poets, Teen Howl, the Carnegie Center, and the Bluegrass Writers Studio.

www.ingramcontent.com/pod-product-compliance
Lightning Source LLC
Chambersburg PA
CBHW021455080526
44588CB00009B/856